IMAGES
of England

BITTERNE

This six inches to one mile map of 1910 shows Bitterne's rural setting before the First World War. The 'village' is clustered around Pound Street and Chapel Street, running either side of the stream. Several country houses can be seen along the hill overlooking Southampton to the west, including Mersham, The Ridge and Bitterne Lodge. Other features of note are the toll on Lances Hill, the hotel (the Red Lion), the inn (The Angel) and the waste ground between Pound Street and West End Road, that later became the Recreation Ground. Bitterne Station and the site of the Roman settlement of Clausentum are just off the map, to the west.

IMAGES
of England

BITTERNE

Compiled by
Bitterne Local History Society

BITTERNE LOCAL HISTORY SOCIETY

TEMPUS

First published 1999
Copyright © Bitterne Local History Society, 1999

Tempus Publishing Limited
The Mill, Brimscombe Port,
Stroud, Gloucestershire, GL5 2QG

ISBN 0 7524 1519 0

Typesetting and origination by
Tempus Publishing Limited
Printed in Great Britain by
Midway Clark Printing, Wiltshire

*Dedicated to the memory of Mr Bob Payne (1925-1999): founder member
and vice-president of our society.*

'Greetings From Bitterne' – a postcard published in around 1908 by Clarence Bealing of Swaythling. It was printed for him in Germany. The left-hand view is of Chapel Street, showing the original Baptist chapel (now the home of Richard Sheaf, secretary of Bitterne Local History Society). West End Road, in the right-hand picture, was laid out as a thirty-foot wide carriageway as a result of the Enclosure Act of 1812. This was the first road in Bitterne to be given an asphalt surface. It ran along a high ridge, with a commanding view to the west over Southampton, and was favoured by the gentry, for whom several large houses were built there.

Contents

Aerial view of Bitterne, looking west towards Southampton, mid-1960s. The fork in the main road is at the centre of the picture, with Bursledon Road running to the bottom left-hand corner and Bitterne Road to the bottom right. The spire of the parish church can be clearly seen, with the schools just visible between the church and the flat-roofed bowling alley. The large wooded area (centre background) is Hum Hole, with the Lances Hill section of the main road to its left, going downhill towards the River Itchen (in the top left-hand corner). The bypass leaves Lances Hill at this point, running through Hum Hole, across the site of the recreation ground (known locally as The Sandpit) and the Congregational chapel (seen on the corner of Dean Road), to join Bursledon Road, where Albert Terrace can be seen. The road running from left to right, between Hum Hole and The Sandpit, is West End Road, which follows the high ridge overlooking Southampton. Also visible in this picture are the modern police station (bottom left), the Roman Catholic church and the library (bottom right), and the 'old' village (over to the right).

Introduction

Britain became an island between 9,000 and 6,000 years ago, when the sea level rose at the end of the last Ice Age and formed what eventually became the peninsula of Southampton. The consequent widening of the River Itchen formed a natural barrier with the eastern land-mass that includes the area today known as 'Bitterne'.

The recorded history of the district begins with the creation (by AD 70) of a well-defended Roman port, known as 'Clausentum', on the eastern bank of the river in the area of the modern Bitterne Manor. A Roman road was constructed from the port to the east, leading to Chichester, but direct communication with the western bank was only possible by ford or boat, making this eastern area fairly isolated. Following the Roman withdrawal in the early fifth century, the Saxon town of Hamwic gradually developed, concentrated in the eastern area of the central peninsula. The subsequent emergence of the large medieval town of Hamtun (that eventually became the modern port of Southampton) was paralleled by the Manor of Byterne on the eastern shore, owned by the wealthy Bishop of Winchester. The modern district of Bitterne Park to the north is an echo of that period. The general area was, and continued to be, a rural district within the County of Hampshire.

The River Itchen remained a natural barrier until 1799, when the first bridge was completed to the bank of Bitterne Manor. This wooden structure gave, for the first time, direct access from the town to the Bitterne area and thus to the eastern part of the county – to Portsmouth in particular. It also gave access to the large private estates and country houses owned by the 'landed gentry' who had taken up residence in this desirable country area. Sadly, few of these estates have withstood the onslaught of property developers over the years. Other bridges followed: Cobden Bridge to the north in 1883 and Itchen Bridge to the south in 1977. The latter replaced the steam-driven (later diesel-powered) floating bridges, established in 1836.

The eastern area was within the County of Hampshire, with its own rural district and parish councils, but in 1895 the Southampton Corporation proposed an extension of the borough boundaries to include, among other parishes, Bitterne. This proposal was vigorously resisted, and a petition was made to Hampshire County Council in 1896, which referred to the independent existence of Bitterne as a village and its preference to remain a separate parish – as created out of South Stoneham in 1894. Further attempts were made, and resisted, until March 1920, when the village was finally incorporated into the Borough of Southampton, along with Sholing, Itchen and Woolston. Harefield remained outside until 1954.

The central Bitterne area retained its 'village' identity for many years, but part of the former High Street is now a pedestrian precinct, with – an unusual feature in modern times – free car parking near the shopping centre. This has served to concentrate interest in the Bitterne district, which remains a focal point for the eastern area. Although the current population of the Bitterne area was recorded as 12,747 in the 1991 census, the entire catchment area (with the adjacent wards) totalled 81,784, thus comprising nearly half of Southampton's total population of almost 197,000.

The Bitterne Local History Society is very much a part of this scene. This society was formed in 1981 and has well over 200 members, some of whom are former residents now living elsewhere in the country or abroad. It was originally composed of local Bitterne residents who met to share old photographs and memorabilia of Bitterne Village. This inner area had remained semi-rural, on the outskirts of Southampton, until after the Second World War, but then gradually lost its original structure, particularly after the construction of the bypass. However, it still retains much of its local character and individuality, with many residents holding strong views on their collective identity. It was this strength of local feeling that rapidly increased the membership of the initial group of residents and led to the formation of the Bitterne Local History Society. Interest and local history research was initially confined to the Bitterne Village area, but over a period of time this has been extended to the neighbouring districts and now includes virtually the entire area of Southampton east of the River Itchen. The aims of the Society are to encourage an active interest in local history, especially amongst students and schools, and to assist in historical research.

From the early days, the members of Bitterne Local History Society had the aim of owning and running a local museum, devoted to items relating to Bitterne and its immediate surroundings. It was with this in mind that artefacts have been steadily collected over the years, providing nostalgic reminders of the old Bitterne Village and its inhabitants. Many items would perhaps be considered as unsuitable for inclusion in a traditional museum, but experience has shown that they nevertheless attract great interest and promote sentimental reminiscences. A selection is currently housed in the Society's Heritage and Research Centre at no. 225 Peartree Avenue, near the heart of the village. The resources, including a collection of over 2,000 photographs and an extensive assortment of research material, are available to all those interested in local history. Facilities and displays are also open for use and viewing by local schools and colleges, who are encouraged to borrow items short-term for 'hands-on' educational purposes. An associated charity shop, a few doors away, finances the Heritage Centre by converting donated items into cash and selling the numerous publications produced by the Society.

The interior of the Heritage and Research Centre, showing part of the study area.

One

Village Life

Nineteenth-century Bitterne Village was a stable and predominately rural community, with a good share of local characters and personalities. The housing was varied but simple and reflected the, generally working-class, background of most residents. The modern spread of urban housing has changed the outlying area considerably, but the basic local character of the community has remained consistent. What better place to start than in the heart of Bitterne Village – which, was centred on the Pound and nearby churches and is now a pedestrian precinct.

The last house on the right in Church View, Pound Street, adjacent to 'The Sandpit', recreation ground, is Mrs Major's shop, with a horse-drawn delivery cart outside. In recent years many such shops have been converted to dwelling houses, with the shop window removed and replaced with a bay window. The Pound was moved shortly after this picture was taken, in around 1904, to make room for the Wesleyan Methodist church. The new site was owned by Captain John Diaper, who, as captain of the Royal Yacht for forty years, taught King Edward VII (then Prince of Wales) to sail. The Pound was a relic from the days when herds of animals were driven through the village, *en route* to market in Southampton. It was last used in 1950 when four calves from Upper Townhill Farm 'broke out' and strayed along Manor Farm Road. They were taken to the Pound for the night and, as in past years, fed by the local police officers.

George Gould and his son, George Henry, *c.* 1920. They were well-known Bitterne undertakers, as well as being house repairers and decorators, a common joint enterprise. They closed in 1935, on the death of George junior, as his wife Lily and daughter 'Dolly' were unable to carry on the business. 'Dolly' would have liked to have done so, but it was not then 'the done thing' for a lady to act as undertaker. This photograph was taken at no. 393 Bitterne Road, formerly known as no. 4 Oak Villas, High Street. The site is now occupied by the Superdrug store.

Ailsa Villas was built in around 1865 and is pictured here in 1884. It was the home of James Brown, butler to the Coote family at Shales, West End Road. Irene Pilson, the well-known author of two books on Bitterne, was born there in 1910. These two villas are now nos 14 and 16 Brook Road and, during the 1960s, were the home of the Cox and West families. In the 1970s, they were used as the set for a TVS children's television programme.

Chapel Street, *c.* 1905. This was so-named because of its three chapels: the Wesleyan (seen in the background), Congregational and the Baptist (which later became Anglican). This section was renamed Dean Road in 1924, four years after Bitterne was incorporated into Southampton.

Chapel Street, *c.* 1913. The original Baptist church (built in 1844) is on the right and the post office, managed by W. Goffe, on the extreme left. The corner shop was run by Nalder Roberts and the sign states 'Tea Dealer and Coffee Roaster'. A projection room was later built on top of the church porch, during its period as Bitterne's first cinema in the 1920s. The combustible nature of silver nitrate film necessitated the projection equipment being outside the auditorium, with the picture projected through a hole in the wall. Despite changes to the road, all three of these buildings remain, as does one of the six trees on the roadside.

White's Rd, Bitterne.

At the time this picture was taken, around 1905, Whites Road was still an unmade road. In this view, looking north towards Bursledon Road, the wall of Brownlow House estate can be seen on the left. This was named after the Very Revd Brownlow North, Bishop of Winchester from 1781 until his death in 1820. Prior to 1839, the road had been part of Bitterne Common and was enclosed, in about 1860, for market gardening. It was named after Whites Estates, who owned much of the land and who opened it up for development in around 1880.

Red Lion Cut, *c.* 1912 . This shows the junction with Bursledon Road. Mrs Gale, pictured with baby Herbert, lived in this cottage, the original Red Lion Hotel. The cut was unofficially referred to as Jordan's Cut and, later, as Godwin's Cut, after the successive owners of the newsagent's shop, halfway along.

Butts Road Brickworks, c. 1926. The people are, from left to right: Alf Chalk and Messrs John, Bill, Les and Charlie Derham – who owned the brickworks. There were a large number of brickworks in the area, including one known as the 'Sheepwash', near the stream in the dip at the junction of modern Deacon and Bursledon Roads, where hand-made bricks were produced until the late 1930s. This was quite an industry in Bitterne, as clay was readily available at the bottoms and sides of the local hills, where it tended to come to the surface. Many Bitterne bricks were used in the construction of the Royal Victoria Military Hospital at Netley, on Southampton Water.

R. Haynes were decorators and repairers in Church Road (later no. 103 Bursledon Road). Their employees, pictured here in around 1914 with Marion Haynes, included two Mr Fishers, S. Biggs, H. Henning, G. Hoskins, R. Haynes and A. Hodkinson. Mrs Haynes was killed when a bomb destroyed the house in the Second World War.

These strawberry pickers are probably on the Brownlow estate, *c.* 1914. The sheltered climate afforded by the Hampshire basin and the Isle of Wight made the region well suited to market gardening and soft fruit cultivation. The strawberry was, and still is, a popular crop locally.

Charles Martin, in his boot and shoe shop at no. 397 Bitterne Road (formerly no. 9 High Street), *c.* 1915. Most of the items of footwear seen in the picture are boots. At that time, almost all men wore boots and many women wore them too, laced up almost to their knees. Shoes became fashionable for ladies after the First World War. Boot repairers were in great demand because everyone walked and, although the soles were real leather and six millimetres thick, the rough terrain wore them through. There was also much demand for repairs to the uppers and every repair shop needed a range of special machines to sew the leather. Charles is seen here using a snob's hammer, but most repairers used a rasp to hammer in the brads. He was known as 'Peggy' Martin, because of his wooden leg. His son Len took over the business in around 1920.

Many residents expanded their home-based 'paying hobbies' into fully developed businesses, especially when they catered for the local big estates. One such entrepreneur was Walter Stratton, who supplied many of the big houses with fruit, flowers and tomatoes (his speciality) from his nursery (Fircroft) at no. 78 Bursledon Road. The entrance was in Lodge Road (now Ruby Road). Mildred Stratton, his daughter, used to take the orders each week to Bitterne Court, on the Bramwell estate, and was always rewarded by the cook with a big brown egg for breakfast. His son Leonard, pictured right with some of the flowers they were renowned for, was for many years a schoolteacher at Woolston and, later, became headmaster of Redbourn School in Hertfordshire. He died in 1971.

Members of the Manchester Unity Independent Order of Oddfellows, Loyal Fleming Lodge No. 4121, at a rally on the Harefield House estate, c. 1918. The fine banner, together with much of their regalia, is stored by Bitterne Local History Society.

Charles Watson was the last resident of Vectis Cottage, the Bitterne School headmaster's house, before it was demolished for a shopping development in 1937. Pupils, as part of their education, used to cut the hedge, with tall boys working at one end and the shorter ones at the other. In the church grounds, adjacent to the school, there was a garden tended by the boys under Mr Watson's tuition and much of the produce was given to them. This would have been a great help to some of the Bitterne families in the depression of the 1920s and early 1930s.

One of the original cottages built beside the stream, No. 57 Chapel Street (now Dean Road), known in the 1920s as Blundell's Cottage. George and Rose Blundell lived in the cottage in Spring Gardens, which lay between the stream behind Lorne House and the old Baptist Chapel.

PC Poore was the earliest known local police officer, working from his cottage in 1851. Shown here is the village's first Hampshire County Police station, erected on the corner of Whites Road and Bursledon Road in 1858. It was subsequently demolished and the present building opened on the same site on 1 March 1965, for Southampton City Police. It reverted to 'County' status on 31 March 1967 when the force amalgamated with the Hampshire Constabulary.

These stalwart Hampshire County (Bitterne) police officers, photographed in around 1920, are commanded by Sergeant Ernest Harry Baugh, who was stationed there from 1912 to 1920. He retired to Lymington and lived well into his nineties. He was succeeded by the first Southampton officer, Sergeant E. Smith, who had come top in the 1920 promotion examination. He chose Bitterne, his home village that had just become part of the Borough, for his initial posting and remained there until 1931.

The 3rd Itchen Cubs, *c*. 1930. This group included 'Kim' Ethel Gordon (Cub Mistress), Jack Hasler, Cyril Line, Johnny Salter, John Freemantle, Harold Smith, Jim Hulbert, John Holt, Ron Hulbert, 'Nodgy' Parsons, 'Soupy' West, Jack Myers and Lennie Noyce. They met at the Martin Hall, Brook Road (renamed Gordon Hall in 1969), built in 1881 by the daughter of Admiral Thomas Martin of Bitterne Lodge.

Bitterne Scouts Bugle Band, *c*. 1921. They are pictured at Bitterne Court in Milbury Crescent, the residence of Miss Bramwell and her family. Boy Scouts first met in Bitterne in September 1908, with two patrols, Peewits and Kangaroos. In June 1909, the troop was registered as the 17th (Bitterne) Southampton, under Scout Master Chas E. Goodwin, with a further two patrols, Cuckoos and Lions. Included are, from left to right, top row: R. Watton, A. Hammerton, H. Watson, C. Defort, Mr Powell (bandmaster), Capt. Roger. Centre row: H. Hooper, A. Russell, S. Bunce, R. Read, V. Osborn, E. Henry and Revd Adams (curate). Bottom row: R. Henry, C. Osborn, A. Porter and G. Brennan.

Kerb layers, c. 1931. The workers are engaged in the making of Gainsford Road on the former Ridgeway House estate. The area was dubbed 'The Garden Suburb' by the agents, Messrs Fox and Sons. Bungalows were offered for sale on a deposit of only £25. Bert Instone is marked with a cross in the centre.

These houses in Bursledon Road were built in the 1920s and cost about £450 each. The 'C. Read' advertising the property lived at No. 104 Bursledon Road and ran a general shop (which later became Sperring's newsagents) in White's Road.

Reuben Cleverley and Frank Cutting in front of Guy's Cottage, which served as the school tuck shop. It was one of the many thatched cottages with cob walls to be found in Bitterne. The front door was reached by means of a plank across an open ditch.

These thatched cottages at Nos 12/14 Pound Street (originally Pound Lane), photographed in around 1940, were known as Emery's Cottages and were built with local bricks. The doors shown here faced away from the road and towards the stream, which flowed between Pound Street and Dean Road. Originally, the stream ran through the school grounds and continued until it reached Millers Pond in Portsmouth Road, Woolston. Most of it is now culverted, although it can still be seen near the leisure centre.

In the early part of the twentieth century, disabled individuals were not given financial aid in the form of a Disability Allowance, or other Social Security benefits. Walter Moody, a picture frame maker who lived in Middle Road, had to fend for himself. He did, however, have the benefit of this ingenious hand-powered vehicle, specially constructed for him after he lost his legs.

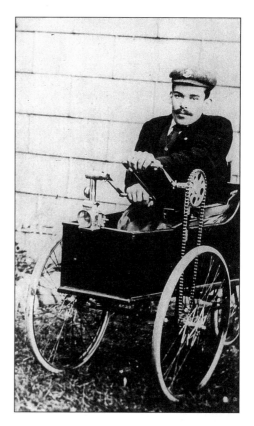

Glenfield Farm in the 1920s, looking east along Mousehole Lane, with the track that was to become Glenfield Avenue leading off to the right.

This photograph was taken on 1 July 1928, by Tom Webb, from the end of Cobden Avenue, looking downhill east along Mousehole Lane. Originally, the road up the hill terminated at this point, with the drive to Bitterne Grove. Between 1881 and 1897, it was extended to join Cobden Avenue. This section is said to have been made up by Welsh miners working under government contract to John Douglas.

Mousehole Lane, looking downhill from Cobden Avenue, c. 1960. Note the cast-iron lamp-posts, old road signs, soft kerbs and absence of yellow lines. Glenfield Farm had now been developed, much of it in the immediate post-war period, when many prefabricated bungalows and houses were built.

This show bungalow was built by Somerset Garden Estates Ltd, who first started to develop the former Harefield House estate in the 1930s. Work ceased on the outbreak of war in 1939 and was subsequently resumed by Southampton Corporation, even though the area remained outside the borough until 1954. The photograph was taken in August 1960, after severe flooding in the valley between Bitterne and Thornhill.

The first post-war rally of the Southampton East Division of the Hampshire Girl Guides was held in 1952 on Bitterne Sports Ground at Hatley Road/Wynter Road. Over 900 members were supported by several hundred parents and friends. Guides from throughout the division took part in a pageant of Guiding, written and devised by Miss Freemantle of Pear Tree Green. The massive canvas backcloth, depicting the Southampton Bargate, was painted by Bob Payne on the roof of his outbuilding, as this was the only place he could accommodate the 24'x 20' former marquee canvas.

Shephard's Cottage, no. 602 Bitterne Road East, which is a Grade II listed building and a unique surviving example of a cob-and-thatch smallholder's cottage within Southampton, still stands at the bottom of the valley to the east of Bitterne. It belonged to the Shephard family, market gardeners in Bitterne for several generations, and is one of the last links with the former rural character of the area. Walter Shephard said that his family had lived there for 300 years! It remains remarkably unaltered from when it was first built with locally available materials.

Spring Place, a terrace of four cottages built at right angles to Chapel Street (now Dean Road), June 1994. A sloping path led to the gates of the garden, where there was a well. The back rooms had bare earth floors and no ceilings, being left open to the slate roof. The two left-hand cottages, Nos 67 and 69, were slate-hung (the first floor of one was over the ground floor of the other!), and were at one time occupied by the Goodfellows and Saits respectively. The Johnsons and Houghtons lived at Nos 71 and 73. The terrace was demolished in 1999.

Two

The Gentry
and Their Homes

The laying of the foundation stone for Southampton Docks in 1838, closely followed by the arrival of the railway, led to the development of Southampton as an ever-expanding commercial port. Many of the gentry came to appreciate the coastal scenery on the eastern side of the River Itchen, away from the bustle of the town, and they developed sizeable estates and country houses in the area. Bitterne, with its fine woodland and commanding views overlooking the town, was ideally suited for these purposes. These estates survived for several generations, until the great social changes following the two world wars brought about their extinction. Although few of the properties or families have survived, they are recalled by the names of the districts and roads, and in photographs that remind us of a bygone age.

The Elizabethan-style Harefield House, photographed in around 1915, was built in 1846 for Sir Edward Butler, the one-time chairman of the Southampton and Salisbury Railway Company. It was set in 238 acres with terraced gardens, an arboretum and ornamental ponds. William Gillett lived there between 1861 and 1885 in some style, introducing a flock of peacocks and building an indoor riding school, subsequently used for village events such as dancing and exhibitions. Edwin Jones, founder of a large Southampton drapery store (now Debenhams), moved into the house in 1889 and lived there until his death in 1896. His widow remarried and continued living there until the house was destroyed by fire on Sunday 6 May 1917.

The medieval Bitterne Manor, occupying the site of the Roman settlement of Clausentum, was owned and used as a farmhouse by the Bishops of Winchester. Later enlarged and refurbished as a private residence, it passed through several owners: from the 1850s it was the family home of Sir Steuart MacNaghten, who was chairman of the Southampton Dock Company from 1869 to 1892. His widow sold the Bitterne Manor estate to the National Land Corporation in 1899 but in 1906 she bought back the house and seven acres. Her daughter, Lettice, continued to live there until 1939. The house was badly damaged by bombing in 1940. Ten years later, the distinguished Southampton architect Herbert Collins bought the derelict property and rebuilt it to provide fourteen private flats.

The conservatory at Bitterne Manor, built around 1805 on the east end of the house. This was when the crenellated façade was added, reflecting the revival of Gothic fashion at the beginning of the nineteenth century.

The wedding of Miss Laura Maud Amy MacNaghten (27), of Bitterne Manor House, to Evelyn Culme-Seymour (26), Lieutenant RN, of 'Glenville', Bitterne, on 29 May 1908. The carriage is travelling down from Bursledon Road past the Red Lion public house. All the children were given a sprig of white heather and a coin (probably a shilling).

Outside Bitterne church, probably on the occasion of the wedding of Kathleen Ada Smith (27), of The Ridge, Bitterne, to Robert Hemphill (27), Captain RAMC, on 30 October 1915. The coachman was Mr Sturgess and the canopy over the church gate was hired from Dyas, blindmakers of Southampton, and erected by local undertaker Mr R.C. Payne.

Ashtown Villa, on the Chessel Estate near the main Chessel House, was once occupied by Lord Ashtown and later called 'Little Chessel'. It had eight and a half acres of land and is pictured here from a 'to be sold or let' advertisement of 1831. This points out that the house 'commands near views of the River Itchen with its extensive scenery around, including the Isle of Wight'.

Chessel House, c. 1920. This was built in 1796 for David Lance, who gave his name to nearby Lances Hill. He had made his fortune with the East India Company, trading to China. The Chessel estate, later surrounded by a long wall, extended from the modern Peartree Avenue to Bitterne Road and the River Itchen.

Chessel Lodge, at the junction of Chessel Avenue and Peartree Avenue. It still stands, although most of the trees have gone and, in 1997 and 1998, rebuilding considerably changed its appearance. This was one of three lodges to the Chessel Estate.

Another Chessel lodge on Lances Hill, c. 1954. This building was subsequently pulled down because of its dilapidated state. The nameplate of Garfield Road can be read in the left foreground. The increase in traffic down Lances Hill led to the closing of this junction, by 1970, for safety reasons (see page 122).

The orangery on the Chessel House estate. Chessel House was built for David Lance in 1796, prior to the opening of Northam Bridge. He was involved with the Company that built it in 1799 (see page 119). Jane Austen, the novelist, was a friend of the Lance family and visited their home several times whilst staying in Southampton. In around 1820, the property was acquired by Lord Ashtown, famous for his futile attempts to convert the Irish to Protestantism.

In times of recession, the landed gentry often found work for idle hands as an act of charity. The wall of Chessel estate was built for this reason in the late 1800s and was commissioned by Chessel's then owner, William Richardson. It extended from what is now the eastern end of the railway bridge, up to Little Lances Hill and to the entrance drive, completely enclosing the estate.

Brownlow Lodge, built in 1906 and named after Brownlow North, former Bishop of Winchester. The site is now occupied by the play-equipment area of Bitterne School. It was once the home of Police Sergeant Burns, of the Hampshire Constabulary. The elaborate chimneys are worthy of note.

Heathfield House, seen with its evergreen magnolia on the wall, was built in around 1830, following the enclosure of old Bitterne Common. It had a succession of owners before becoming a private hotel in the 1930s. Later, it became a nursing home. The iron veranda on the west side was a later addition. A bell on the stable block and staff quarters (still to be seen today in Montgomery Road) was used to summon staff from the grounds.

Shales, West End Road, seen from the tennis courts, *c.* 1884. The house was occupied by Sir Charles Henry Coote from around 1850 until he sold it to his brother, Admiral Robert Coote, in 1865. It was then owned successively by Col. Bald (in around 1888), Col. Perkins and Redcote Convent. Renamed Langstaff House and then, finally, St Theresa's, it was demolished in around 1970. St Francis House and St Theresa House (sheltered accommodation) were built on the site.

Members of the Coote family at Shales, *c.* 1885. They are, from left to right (front row only): Stanley Victor Coote, Mrs Lucy Coote (his mother), Admiral Robert Coote, M.C. Mann and C.G. Robinson. Standing at the back are Cecil William Park and his wife Caroline Maud, the Admiral's daughter.

The Shales drawing room is typical of Victorian country houses, *c.* 1885. The profusion of ornaments did not involve Mrs Coote, the Admiral's wife, in excessive household duties as she had an abundance of house servants, albeit without modern electrical appliances.

Admiral Robert Coote, CB, JP, at his home, Shales, West End Road. Similar uniforms are still worn today on formal occasions, although this photograph looks as if it could have been taken after a modern performance of *HMS Pinafore*! He was born at Geneva on 1 June 1820, the fourth son of Sir Charles Henry Coote, the ninth baronet, and was educated at Eton. In 1833, aged thirteen, he entered the Navy and, by 1854, had reached the rank of captain. As the captain of HMS *Victory* at Portsmouth, from March 1860 to March 1863, he organised the new Naval Police. He was appointed rear admiral in 1870. The honour of Companion of the Order of the Bath followed in 1873 and he was Commander-in-Chief Coast of Ireland, from January 1874 to June 1876, when he became vice admiral. He was Commander-in-Chief China from 1878 to 1881, when he was made full admiral, retiring in 1885. He died at 'Arden', College Road, Dulwich, on 17 March 1898, and was buried in Brookwood Cemetery.

The stables at Shales, photographed on 25 October 1885. One of the men in the picture is the coachman, Patrick Ahern, then aged thirty-eight, who was a widower born in Bruff, Ireland.

The 1881 Census lists the following servants at Shales: James Brown (the butler, standing extreme left with the fine hat), Charlotte Stow (lady's maid), Sarah Smith (the cook, sitting front left), Sarah Duckett (upper housemaid), Alice Wellstead (under housemaid), Alice Lambden (kitchen maid), Joseph Parsons (footman) and Patrick Ahern (coachman). There were, no doubt, several others not living in, as other names are recorded on this picture, taken in around 1884.

Rap and Shot, *c.* 1886. These were two pets, belonging to the Coote family at Shales. A family album of 1884 to 1886, now held by Bitterne Local History Society, contains many photographs of these dogs, which were clearly much loved. This photograph, showing a poster detailing the Rabies Order of 1886, was obviously a family joke, although such posters had to be displayed by law. Over a century later, countering rabies with quarantine regulations is still making the news.

Parishes were grouped together into Poor Law unions, each responsible for the care of the poor within their jurisdiction. The South Stoneham Union built an extensive workhouse in West End and this picture, of around 1885, shows a party of girls from there on an outing to Shales. This workhouse is now Moorgreen Hospital and the building's former usage still fills older residents with a dread of 'going into Moorgreen'.

Moorlands was once the residence of Sir Richard Glass, a pioneer of submarine cables. The 124 acre estate was owned by the Sholto-Douglas family from 1893 until it was auctioned for development in 1919. When the house was demolished, part of the banister was salvaged for use as an altar rail in the parish church. The lodge to the estate still stands on the corner of West End Road and Hood Road.

Staff of the Bitterne Court estate, which occupied the area bounded by Bitterne Road, Bursledon Road and Bath Road, where Milbury Crescent and Court Close now stand. It was sold to the builder John Nicol in 1923 for £2,500. However, he did not develop it and his executors sold the estate, for £8,000, to property developers Milbury Estates in the 1930s. Included in the picture are Teddy Trodd, Mr Boyce, Harry Othen, and Sarah, the cook.

36

Replacing an old farm house, Townhill Park House was built as a country mansion in 1793 for Nathaniel Middleton, a 'nabob' who had done well in India. It later belonged to the Gater family, from whom it was bought, in around 1897, by Sir Samuel Montagu (who was created Baron Swaythling in 1907). His eldest son, Louis, who succeeded him in 1911, had the old house attractively rebuilt and enlarged, to the design of L. Rome Guthrie, before and after the First World War. When the 324 acre estate was sold off, in 1948, the house, together with thirty acres, was purchased by Middlesex (later Hounslow) education authority for use as a special school. In 1969, Southampton City Council acquired it to accommodate marine engineering cadets. Transferred to Hampshire County Council in 1974, this hostel later became redundant and the house was sold in 1994 to The Gregg School.

The wonderful gardens of Townhill Park House, photographed in March 1950, were originally laid out by the celebrated landscape gardener Gertrude Jekyll in the 1920s. They are currently being restored to their former splendour by the Friends of Townhill Park House & Gardens and the Hampshire Gardens Trust.

Peartree House, built in the late sixteenth century, was owned and occupied by the Mylles family until 1780, when it passed to relatives, with whom it remained until 1828. General Shrapnel, inventor of the shrapnel shell, bought it in 1835 and lived there until his death in 1842. Southampton Corporation acquired it in 1949 as an old people's home. This was closed in 1996 and the house is now a private specialist rehabilitation nursing home.

Midanbury Castle was, in fact, the gatekeeper's lodge of the Midanbury Estate. The mansion itself, Midanbury Lodge, first appears on a 1791 map. It had various owners, including the Southampton merchant Michael Hoy from 1815 to 1827, and (following his death) his nephew, the MP James Barlow, who changed his name to Hoy. The lodge was empty and derelict from 1913 until it was demolished in the 1930s to make way for the Castle Inn. There have been various spellings of Midanbury, including Maidenbury, Midannbury, and Middanbury.

Three

Traders
and Public Houses

As Bitterne Village grew, so did its need for the essential services provided by local traders and craftsmen. The gentry, with their splendid estates, also required products and services for their staff and guests. England was once derided by Napoleon as being 'a nation of shopkeepers' and Bitterne was no exception to this national characteristic. All needs, as they arose, were catered for, with the native shrewdness of many locals exploiting every situation. Many initially traded from their home and, as their businesses prospered, expanded into purpose-built or adapted premises. They, in turn, together with the servants and workers, with their limited leisure and finances, sought the relaxation and pleasure of public houses in their off-duty time – this need was also catered for in no small measure. All these activities combined to weld Bitterne Village into a close-knit community, with its own special identity.

Bitterne post office, *c.* 1916. This was in Chapel Street, at the shop owned by W. Goffe, who was also a stationer and newsagent. On the left are the carriage premises of 'Carey, Fly Proprietor' (who hired out horse-drawn vehicles).

Bunney's shop at No. 2 Brook Road, in March 1926, with Mrs Bunney, her grandsons and son, Reg. They gave their name to a part of Chichester Road that villagers called 'Bunney's Hill'. The shop was spotlessly maintained, with a gleaming mahogany counter, sweet cabinet and shining glass jars.

The premises of Alexander Cardy, beer retailer, in Commercial Street, on the corner of York Drove, *c.* 1900. Pictured here, from left to right, are: Alice Cardy, Blanche Cardy (both daughters of Alexander), Rose Cardy (wife of Alexander's son Edgar) and their dog, Bullar. Alexander was also landlord of the Yew Tree public house, on the opposite side of the road, where Haynes Road now runs.

Lane's Bakery, No. 88 Commercial Street, opposite the junction of Almatade Road, *c.* 1915. Residents could take their home-made cakes to be baked in the oven in this shop. An oven door from this bakery is in the Bitterne Local History Society collection.

William Cane, baker and confectioner of Chapel Street, *c.* 1912. The St John's Hall now stands approximately on this site. The delivery van, with Arthur and Frank Knowlton, is pictured in York Drove.

The Angel Inn, *c.* 1895. An old coaching inn, it was only two storeys high, but a dummy front gave the impression of a much larger building. On the right is one of Mr Whicher's carriages, which could be hired from No. 3 Oak Villas (opposite). The building was demolished in 1972 for an expansion to Sainsbury's supermarket.

The Bitterne Station Hotel, *c.* 1915. This is close to the Bitterne railway station. Mr Rockett's horse-drawn wagon and the motor taxicab, together with the overhead tramcar wires visible over the road, show the mix of transport that co-existed at this time. Mr Rockett held a contract for the transport of goods from the railway to the village. The hotel was once the property of the local Cobden Bridge Brewery, which was taken over by Fuller, Smith and Turner's Brewery in 1898. This company was itself taken over by Courage in November 1920 for £8,000.

The Red Lion Stables, *c.* 1905. This was an important staging post on the main road east from Southampton. A 'stage' in coaching terms was usually about eight miles, but the Southampton to Bitterne stage was less to make allowance for the steep incline of Lances Hill. For the larger, horse-drawn coaches and other large goods wagons, horses were kept at the foot of the hill and they could be hired to assist in pulling the load up. Among the group here is Mr Gale, who was employed as a chaff-cutter and lived in Red Lion Cut. The coachman was probably Mr Mist.

The Red Lion, photographed here on 21 September 1931, was built in the 1860s, although the bay windows were added later. This building replaced the original Red Lion (see page 12), which had opened in the 1830s, with F. Brooks as landlord. Formerly owned by Coopers Brewery, it later became a Watney's house. It was refurbished in 1995 and is still a popular public house, serving fine food.

H.J. Boyes' bakery, at No. 413 Bitterne Road (formerly No. 25 High Street), *c.* 1933. The Morris van is driven by Wesley G. Brown, who was delivery driver from 1914 to 1939. The roof repair being carried out was due to the chimney stack being blown off in a gale. During the 1920s and '30s, there was a tearoom at the back of the shop. Bitterne school children would buy a stale bun (i.e. baked yesterday) for a ha'penny instead of a penny.

Mrs Martha (Granny) Godwin is pictured here, aged eighty, outside her newspaper shop in Red Lion Cut, *c.* 1915. She still ran the shop and served in it regularly when she was over 100 years old. In 1933, when she was ninety-eight, she was described in the *News of the World* as the oldest newsagent in Britain. She always dressed in black and wore a lace cap, such as was favoured by Queen Victoria. When she retired, Mr and Mrs Harry Fraser took over the shop until it was demolished, in the early 1980s, to facilitate work on the bypass. At the time of their retirement, they were still using the gas lighting in emergencies and showing £. s. d. on the till – eleven years after decimalization.

The 1947 Christmas display of Horlock and Son, butchers, at the corner of Brook Road and Pound Street. Between the wars, the triangular piece of land bounded by West End Road, Pound Street and Chichester Road, was known as The Rookery because of the number of rooks that used to roost there in the tall trees. These were culled by Mr Horlock's sons (rook pie was considered a delicacy around the village). By the time the shop closed, in the 1980s, it had been a butchers for over a century.

Minns Drapers, c. 1908. This was located on the corner of High Street and Pound Street, adjacent to White's hairdressers and Martin's boot repairers. The premises later became Southwell's dairy shop, and then Lloyds Bank, who are still there, although the building has been rebuilt.

Benhams Farm, viewed from higher up Witts Hill *c*. 1905. There were several Benhams living in the parish of South Stoneham early in the nineteenth century and some members of the family worked the farm. Previously forming part of Mousehole Lane, Witts Hill was renamed after William Witt, who occupied the farm in Victorian times. Benhams was primarily a dairy farm, although it also had piggeries. The building on the hill in the background is Moorlands.

Mr Petty at Benhams Farm, *c*. 1935. Alfred Brown's main dairy was Hill Farm in Hill Lane, Shirley. The firm merged with Harrison's in 1940, who in turn were taken over in 1957 by South Coast Dairies (now part of Unigate). The farmhouse still exists, albeit as a private residence, but the outhouses, cowsheds and piggeries were demolished for the development of Benhams Farm Close by the Swaythling Housing Association in 1996.

Mr Boyce and Mr J. Hounsell of Southwell's Dairy, at the bottom of Whites Road, c. 1920. Mr Lewis Owen Southwell began business in 1916 on the corner of Pound Street, where Miss Minns had formerly run her haberdashery business, on the site now occupied by Lloyds Bank. Two deliveries a day were then the norm and bottled milk (with cardboard discs on a wide-necked bottle) did not arrive until 1927. Although some milkmen had a pony and cart, most, like Mr Southwell, pushed a heavy hand-cart, usually on gravel roads. The milkman would carry a heavy pewter milk can to each house, where the housewife would already have her jug(s) ready, for a pint or half-pint to be measured out. The business was sold to Alfred Brown Ltd in 1932.

Cliff Godwin and his son, Neville, pictured outside their home in Whites Road, c. 1929. He was in partnership with George Ball at no. 433 Bitterne Road, but they split after a short time and Mr Ball carried on until the 1980s. They were renowned for their quality Danish bacon, with bulk deliveries made every Monday at mid-day.

R.C. Payne and Son, undertakers, established 1887. Western Place was a terrace in Commercial Street, adjacent to York Drove, now the Percy Arms car park.

S.A. Harding, confectioner, tobacconist, grocer and fruiterer. Many such corner shops were built with an angled corner, to provide a highly visible location for an advertising hoarding. The advertisers, R.C. Payne, took over these premises when Sid Harding moved to Brighton in 1932. They sold paint, wallpaper and other decorating materials from here (their undertaking business at this time still operated from premises further up Commercial Street). Bitterne Local History Society were able to display some of their collection and sell local publications from here in the 1980s, courtesy of Bob Payne, who did much to further the aims of the Society. The next shop to the right, along Bitterne Road, was Mills and Austin's cycle repairs. This shop is now incorporated into R.C. Payne's premises. Mr Mills left the partnership soon after this picture was taken, but Mr Austin carried on until November 1969.

Mr Robert Chapman Payne, pictured in the workshop of his premises on the corner of Commercial Street in the late 1970s. As well as continuing in the family firm of undertakers, he was a talented signwriter, who was responsible for many of the village shop signs. He also produced posters for the Congregational (United Reformed) church, of which he was a member from 1913 until he died in 1982 – a total of sixty-nine years. He served variously as treasurer and life deacon, as well as carrying out much of the maintenance of the premises over the years – on many occasions at no cost to the church . He believed in diversity, as one of his visiting cards shows him to be a decorator, plumber, gasfitter, house agent, insurance agent and undertaker, as well as a signwriter!

Coal deliveries were an essential service before the days of electric and gas heating, when all cooking and washing was done using solid fuels. The work was hard, not only because of having to carry the hundredweight sacks on the back, but it also involved tending the horse, keeping the yard stacked up and the sacks damped down to avoid too much dust in customers' homes. The coal merchant ordered his supplies from the pits in the North or Wales and it was his responsibility to collect them from the railway station. If he was late, he could be charged rent for the rail wagon which was holding his load. Andrews is a local firm still operating, albeit without the horses, but Bitterne and Woolston stations lost their coalyards many years ago.

Bitterne Brewery, c. 1920. This was a public house and not a brewery in the usual sense of the word. The building was severely damaged by enemy action on 22 June 1942 and the landlord, Mr William J. Sly, was fatally injured. It was rebuilt and became a popular place for parties and for group meetings – including the local Labour Party and the Young Men's Group – until closure in 1998. The garages on the left were the home of the Queen and Hiawatha charabancs. One of Bitterne's earlier pubs, The Star, stood behind the Brewery (where Tenby Close now stands).

The Firs Inn, a public house from the early 1870s, when William Wyatt was the licensee. Note the wooden scaffolding in use during some construction work. The building itself was considerably older, originally being owned by John Sennatt, who founded the first Wesleyan chapel in a cottage at the rear in 1806. Once the property of Aldridge's Bedford Brewery, The Firs later belonged to the Portsmouth Brewers, Brickwoods, and then Whitbread, until closure and demolition in 1974. It was a small, one-room pub and the beer glasses were filled straight from the barrels, which lay on trestles behind the bar. The site is now occupied by Stuart Bridgewater House.

T.J. Stokes in Lion Place, No. 458 Bitterne Road (formerly No. 44 High Street), *c.* 1912. He was in business as a boot and shoe supplier from 1887 to 1924. His garage was the first Congregational Sunday School, established as a 'daughter' Sunday school of the Above Bar Congregational church in 1851. At Christmas, 1917, hand-made boots were advertised from 3/6d to 8/6d a pair. The picture shows, from left to right: Winnie White, Elizabeth Stokes, Thomas James Stokes and Herbert Charles White. Mr Stokes lived to be a centenarian.

The former T.J. Stokes premises, now H.C. White's (Mr Stokes' nephew), *c.* 1926. This is proudly advertised as a 'Boot and Shoe Warehouse', with Mr H.C. White and Mr T.J. Stokes. The business continued from 1925 to 1957, when Mr White retired.

Staff of Lankester and Crook. County Supply Stores, part of Lion Place in Bitterne Road, *c.* 1939. They were founded in 1855 by Mr Lankester in Obelisk Road, Woolston, becoming Lankester and Spencer in 1880 and, when Mr Spencer retired in 1890, Lankester and Crook. They styled themselves as 'Grocers, wine and spirit merchants, butchers, bakers, ironmongers & etc.' with branches in Woolston, Bitterne Park, Portswood, Shirley, Netley, Portsmouth, Titchfield and Waterlooville. It was the supermarket of its day and gave a high standard of personal service.

Lion Place, High Street, Bitterne, *c.* 1905. This was taken after part of the frontage had been reconstructed to create a single large shop for the Lankester and Crook County Supply Stores.

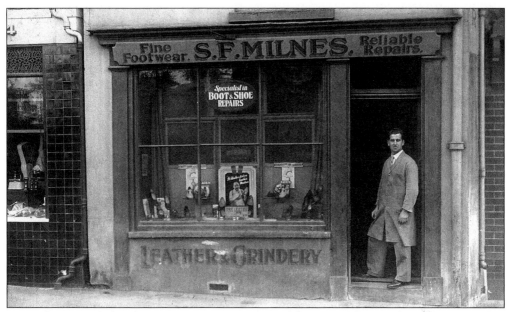

S.F. Milnes outside his shop at No. 482 Bitterne Road (no. 64 High Street), *c*. 1936. Note that they traded in 'Leather and Grindery' – they were originally saddlers. The door to his workshop had a glass panel through which you could watch him work. Stan was an active member of the Congregational Church. The business ran from 1927 to 1976.

May's family butchers, No. 484 Bitterne Road (No. 66 High Street), *c*. 1925. Mr May served the carriage trade and greatly relied on his deliveries to the local gentry. These premises originally had their own slaughterhouse and paddock for cattle and the butcher would, literally, butcher livestock on the premises. BLHS member Mildred Russell records that her grandfather, Edwin Goodall, came to Bitterne from Fareham in the late 1880s and was employed by May's as a slaughterman until the 1920s. These premises were demolished in 1983 during the development of the bypass. The photograph shows Mr Minns, who followed Mr May in the business.

A Redcote Convent laundry delivery van of the 1920s, with Joseph Smeeth and Charlie Dewey. The Redcote blue and orange laundry van was a familiar sight around the district until well into the 1960s. Before becoming a convent in 1901, Redcote House had been the home of Bitterne's first vicar, the Revd Henry Usborne, until his retirement in 1887.

The Lances Hill garage, c. 1938. This was very small compared with garages today and was solely for the sale of motor fuel and oils. It was common practice for the vehicle to pull up at the roadside for the attendant to fill the tank. There was sufficient profit to make a living from the fuel, even at the advertised price of 1s 4d per gallon. The garage closed because it was deemed no longer safe to have the cars stop and for the fuel to be delivered by hose across the pavement. The last proprietor was Mr Jack White, who was an enthusiastic motorcycle 'rallyist'. Holdens Seed and Corn Merchants subsequently traded from here for many years, until replaced by the Black Horse Estate Agents.

Bitterne Parade, *c.* 1935. This was built by Jenkins and Sons Ltd in Bitterne Road, opposite the Red Lion. The sign 'Bitterne Parade' was removed in 1940 during the invasion scare and never replaced. The timbered building on the right was Hornby's dairy. This was once a thriving parade of small shops, including Glanvilles (hairdressers), Dewhurst (butchers) and John Hayton (greengrocers).

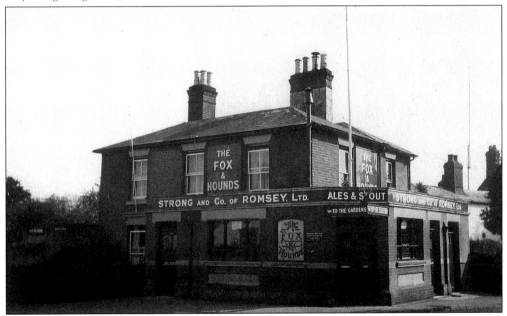

The Fox and Hounds, on the corner of Pound Street and Chichester Road, opened as the Cooper's Arms in the early 1870s, with Robert Boyce as landlord. The name was changed in the 1880s by the then landlord, John Taplin – who was a hunt follower – to honour the local fox-hunt, whose members used to meet there: both the Mersham and Harefield estates had kennels. The Bitterne Brass Band also met there in the 1890s.

No. 225 Peartree Avenue, *c.* 1955. This has become the Bitterne Local History Society Heritage and Research Centre, since 1993. Mr Malcolm Jones traded here from 1954 to 1972, as a grocer, and the shop then became Bitterne photographers (proprietor George Smith). The lady in the picture is Mrs Christina Conley.

The closure of Broomfield and Gatehouse's cycle shop, on 13 August 1988. The sign in the window states 'First and Last Sale'. The name sign over the shop is now in the BLHS Heritage and Research Centre. The Mayor of Southampton, Councillor Pat Bear, is making a presentation to Ted Broomfield and Bert Gatehouse. The building was formerly occupied by Cyril John Hampshire, coal merchants and furniture removers (a wonderful combination of services). It has now been converted into residential accommodation, as No.17 Almatade Road.

Four

Care of Mind and Body

In the early nineteenth century, national education for the working classes was mainly in the hands of Church organisations. Children usually first learnt to read and write at Sunday School or at schools set up as charitable organisations. During the 1840s, such a 'charity school' was provided for the people of Bitterne by Alexander Hoyes of Bitterne Grove. Other schools followed, such as private schools at Monte Repos, High Street, and in Commercial Street, a boys' school at Rustic House (later named Bitterne House), and a girls' school at Albert Villa. An infants' school at the corner of Inkerman (Marne) Road and Commercial Street was funded by the Revd H. Usborne and his sister in 1857. The Education Act of 1870 set up a national system of primary education to replace or supplement the sometimes inharmonious co-existence of Church and non-conformist schools. Locally-elected school boards were given powers to levy rates and build schools, and a further Education Act of 1902 made county and county borough councils the local authorities for elementary and secondary education. All these changes resulted in an expansion of educational resources for the Bitterne area, a process that continues to the present day.

Bitterne Boys' School, Standard V, *c.* 1883. George Henry Gould (see photograph on page 10) is marked with a cross. The master is Mr Henry William Cooke, who became headmaster in August 1873 and retired, after forty-five years' service, in August 1918.

Bitterne School infants, *c.* 1925. They are in their cramped classroom with the old, long gallery seats. It was partitioned off from other classes by a movable screen. Their timid, almost frightened, appearance indicates they were under stern instructions to remain still for the photographer!

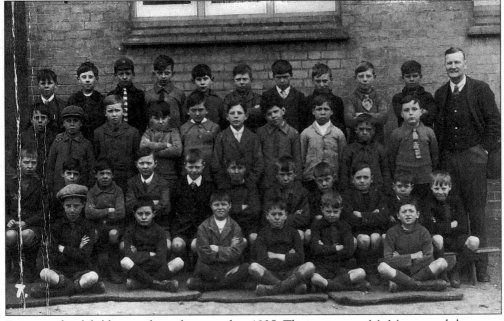

Bitterne schoolchildren in their playground, *c.* 1925. The master was Mr Mercer and the group includes: Ron Haynes, Jon Gale, George Parker, George Hull, ? Parsons, ? Parcell, ? Emery; ? Williams, ? Fisher, ? Dymott, ? Randall-Cole, ? Chalk and ? Barratt.

It appears that all classes had this card for Christmas 1924 (no other years have been found). Note the facial expressions! His Majesty's Inspector's report for this year stated that 'it is difficult adequately to warm the extreme ends of the rooms'.

Bitterne Girls' School children, *c.* 1920. From left to right, back row: Miss Houghton, Sylvia Shepherd, Freda Noyce, Irene Williams, Gladys Oakley, Una Shave. Middle row: Ella Cole, Betty Powell, Vera Goodfellow, Phyllis Dann, Amy Lawrence, Ruby Davey, Dora Birch, Cicely Smart and Violet Hulbert. Front row: I. Rockett, Nellie Dawkins, Nellie Holt, Nellie Winter, Kathleen Prickett, Cherry Prickett, Vera Berry, L. Rockett, Winnie Shepherd, I. Smart, and Vera Missellbrook.

Ex-Army huts were erected on the Middle Road site in 1919, to accommodate Itchen Secondary School before the erection of permanent buildings began in 1926. Some huts remained in use for over forty years! Bitterne Local History Society hold the original building plans for the school.

St Mary's College in the mid-1920s. The original house (the white stucco façade of which can be seen on the left) was Bitterne Grove. It was one of the largest houses in the area, built in around 1790 by Richard Leversuch. He sold it to James Dott, an eccentric who is wrongly reputed to have given us the word 'dotty'. He lived there from 1791 to 1843 and gave refuge to the French aristocrat, the Comte de Cartrie, employing him as a gardener.

The old gym at St Mary's College, built in the early 1930s but demolished since the Second World War. The master in the photograph, taken around 1934, is Brother Arthur, a Frenchman who came to England after teaching in Maine, USA. Brother Arthur, who taught maths and science as well as physical training, drew admiration for his 'pupil pyramids' on Sports Day, a big social event at the college during the 1930s.

The White House and the chapel of St Mary's College. Note that the roof has been altered, since the earlier photograph was taken, to give an extra floor. The inscription over the porch reads 'Thy Kingdom Come'.

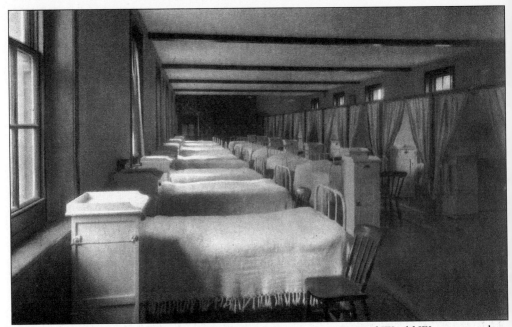

This postcard of a dormitory at St Mary's College depicts a pre-Second World War scene, when the Roman Catholic school took boarders as well as day boys. With the fall of France, it was thought safer to send the boarders to the Order's school at Market Drayton, Shropshire, which remained a boarding school until the 1960s: boarders never returned to St Mary's. An interesting point is that the lockers shown were made by one of the masters, Brother Alpege, a French-Canadian.

The staff of Merry Oak School, c. 1936. The first part of the school opened on 1 April 1935, with the full-scale official opening following on 1 May 1936. Shown here are, from left to right, standing: Messrs Edwards, Ward, Fulton, Nicholls, Lewry, Paul, Nobbs and Ford. Sitting: Misses Domoney, Streatfield, Hayward, Fearne, Mr Permain, Misses Rees, Stout and Duncan.

A Merry Oak School classroom laid out for a meal as part of a domestic science lesson. The first teacher of this subject was Miss G.M. Rees. She was replaced in 1938 by Miss Mary Malpas, who remained until the girls were transferred from Merry Oak School to Sholing Girls' School in July 1945.

A domestic science lesson in a well-equipped classroom, with Rosslyn Parker, Emily Lewis, Vera Pye and Sylvia McCalla. When the girls left the school in 1945, it became Merry Oak Secondary Modern Boys' School. It closed in 1986 and now only the former school hall remains (used as a local community centre).

Alderman Lyons, Ted Ford (headmaster) and the Mayor of Southampton watching Horace King planting a commemorative tree at Merry Oak School on 25 February 1967. Former head of English at Taunton's School and headmaster of Regents Park Boys' School, Horace King was an MP for over twenty years, representing both Test and Itchen constituencies, the last six as Speaker of the House of Commons. He was made a life baron in 1971, adding Maybray to his title (as there was already a Lord King). He lived in Bitterne Park for most of his life and died in 1986, aged eighty-five, shortly after the Bitterne bypass was named after him.

Bitterne School canteen, bedecked for a Christmas party with Santa Claus, 1955. Bitterne School was one of the first schools in Southampton to have dining facilities.

Queen of the May on the Vicarage Lawn, with Peggy Harding, Doris Jeans, Kathy Russell, Elsie Grant and Nancy West, *c.* 1932. Many schools and villages celebrated May Day, the coming of Spring, with a traditional Maypole dance.

Bitterne School Maypole Group. This was a postcard sent by Miss K. Sharman (headmistress), on 11 September 1909 to Miss Berry, School House, Netheravon, Salisbury. Miss Sharman is shown at the right of the picture. Maypole dancing has not completely died out locally – children at Harefield Infants School still learn some of the dances, although not on such a grand scale.

Games in the playground of Bitterne School, *c.* 1950. This image illustrates the various types of building that made up the school. Here can be seen two Nissen huts of 1940 vintage, with the post-war canteen between them.

The derelict Bitterne School, vacated in July 1978, when the school transferred to new buildings on the Brownlow site. The Junior School, built in 1856 in yellow brick, is centre and right, while to the left is the Queen Victoria Infant School, built in 1897 of the more common local red brick. Suggestions that part of the school be retained for community use never came to fruition and following its demolition new shops, with a church above, were built on the site.

Five

Spiritual Enlightenment

Apart from a Wesleyan congregation, founded in 1806 by twenty-one year old John Sennatt and which met at his home in Pound Street (until a move to their chapel built in Chapel Street in 1823), there is no evidence of other church activity before the middle of the nineteenth century. Bitterne's parish church, the church of the Holy Saviour, was built in Bursledon Road in 1853. The population of Bitterne was then about 1,400. A Congregational church was opened in Commercial Street in 1863 and replaced in 1897 by a new building on the corner of Chapel Street and High Street. These places of worship were well supported and became a very important part of Bitterne Village life. Churches of other denominations and persuasions followed during the early twentieth century and, despite the modern trend of reduced congregations, they continue to give moral guidance in Bitterne Village affairs.

The Monastery of Our Lady of Charity, c. 1935. This was built in 1858 as the Redcote Vicarage for the Revd Henry Usborne, Bitterne's first vicar. Joseph Stewart Cockerton sold it in 1904 to a branch of the Catholic order and the nuns operated a laundry there until the 1960s. It was demolished in around 1970 and most of the estate was sold for the development of Redcote Close and April Close, a transaction which financed the rebuilding of the Convent.

The Wesleyan Methodist chapel in Chapel Street (Dean Road), c. 1900. A river bed under the site was discovered during its construction. It stood opposite the modern Haynes Road until bought and demolished in 1906 by Councillor John Brown, who lived next door and who 'recycled' the bricks. The Wesleyan Methodists then moved to their new church on the corner of the High Street and Pound Street. This was, in turn, vacated when the present Methodist church was built in Whites Road in 1969.

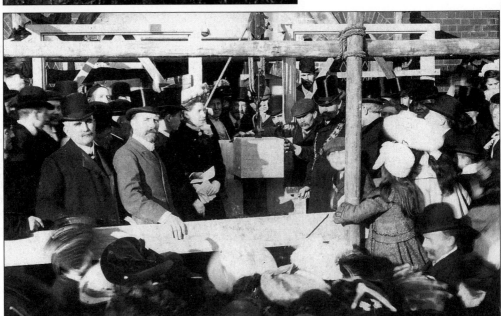

The weather was glorious on Easter Monday, 16 April 1906, when Wesleyan Methodists gathered for the stone-laying ceremony of their new church in Pound Street. Stones were laid by Revd W. Jackson, Revd G. Herbert East, Messrs Warner, F. Houghton, L. Hague, G. Batt, W. Goffe, W.H. Woolf, A.E. Hendy, T. Hedges, G. Harris, and Mesdames E. Russell, Mears, H. Spranklin, and G. Woodford. A number of bricks were also laid by Sunday School scholars.

The Wesleyan Methodist church, c. 1910. The Pound was moved along Pound Street to make room for this building. Mrs Guy's thatched cottage can be seen to the right of the church and Hornby's Dairy, with the roof ridge of the Congregational chapel, behind it. Capt. Diaper of Pound Street paid for the re-building of the Pound and gave ten gold sovereigns to the parish priest to maintain it.

A soup kitchen outside the Wesleyan Methodist church in Pound Street, 1906 David Lloyd George declared in September of this year that 'Britain is the richest country under the sun yet it has ten million workmen living in conditions of chronic destitution. Sixty per cent of the poverty is caused by the imprudent habits of gambling and drink'.

Bitterne Methodists *c.* 1930. The occasion is the Sunday School anniversary, held at The Paddock (Miss Temple's residence), West End Road. From left to right, standing: Mark Macham, Fred Shergold, J. Shergold, R. Pomeroy, H. Smith. Seated: Reg Shergold, E. Pomeroy, P. West, A. Palmer, W. Light, ? West.

Hilltop Youth Club, *c.* 1948. It met at the Bitterne Methodist Hall from 1946 to 1949. Amongst the group are: Vera Hobbs, Harold Blackmore, George Hooper, Arthur Downer, Geoffrey Somerville, Joan Mew, Mrs Whitewell, Jean Johnson, Mr W. Bennett (youth officer), Revd Lewis, Mr F.L. Freeman (chief education officer), Roy Martin, Mr Whitewell, Doris Dee, Rosemary Light, David Whitewell, Maurice Brewer, June Fry, Edith White, Molly Mew, Peter Bell, Maurice Barfoot, Jack Harris and Gwen Reeves.

The 16th Southampton Company Methodist Church Girls Brigade, including: Muriel Fairs, Diane Osman, Ena Light and Wendy Shergold.

The 6th Southampton Methodist Church Boys Brigade, c. 1932. This group existed from 1923 until 1939. The officers in front are, from left to right: J. Callaway, M. Macham, E. Pomeroy, J. Shergold, T. Bunday, W. Johnson and S. Johnson.

An early view (possibly around 1900) of the Congregational church, built in 1897 by Witt Brothers, on the corner of Chapel Street and High Street, at a cost of £1,056. Note the large gas light over the porch. Vivian & Son charged £47 for their gas services and fittings. Seating was provided by the Southampton Steam Joinery Company for £120. The church was built on land used for growing potatoes and compensation for the crop came to £5! The foundation stone on the left was saved when the building was demolished and re-laid in 1986 at the entrance of the United Reformed church in Bitterne Precinct. The previous Congregational church was built in Commercial Street in 1863, replacing a small hall built in 1854.

The Congregational church centenary in 1963. From left to right, front row: Mrs Pook, Revd R.H. Mills, Revd Hugh Jones, Mr S. Learmouth and Mrs Boxall. Back row: Mr E. Joyce, Mr B. Baverstock, Miss D. Norris, Mr R.C. Payne, Mr C.M. Williams, Mrs M. Dawson, Mr A. Law and Mr A. Abraham.

The Band of Hope was an organisation for teaching children the virtues of teetotalism. Meetings were held at a local hall with games, and outings arranged to encourage the children to join. This group includes Miss Abrey, Alice Grant, and Beatrice Knight.

Bitterne Congregational Church Men's Fellowship, c. 1955. They are performing a comedy sketch – *The SS Naughtiness*. The minister in the top hat is the Revd R.H. Mills, and included in the group are: Sid Philpott, Bob Payne, ? Law, ? Pook, E. Joyce, G. Frettingham, Harry Downer, ? Baverstock and ? Mann.

The Congregational schoolroom, just after it was built in 1939 by R.W. Dowman of Bittterne Park, at a cost of £1,300. The hall, which measured fifty feet by twenty-five feet, was opened by Mrs Thornycroft Donaldson. The minister at the time was the Revd C.W. Wall.

The church of the Holy Saviour was built in 1853 by William Gambling on land that was already being used as a burial ground (the earliest grave is dated 1841). The first vicar, the Revd Henry Usborne, and his sister were the main contributors towards the cost. The nave and north aisle are in Gothic style, in Portland stone, with a 120ft high octagonal spire mounted on a tower forming the porch. The Hoyes Memorial Clock was given by Sir Steuart MacNaghten in 1868, in memory of Miss Janet Hoyes of Yew Tree Cottage, Mousehole Lane.

Bitterne church, looking from the south side, *c.* 1908. The south aisle, identical to the north, was added in 1887 (by Woolston builders Chapman) to serve the increasing local population.

An interior view of the church of the Holy Saviour, before the gas lighting was replaced by electric. There were 423 seats originally reserved for the use of the poor, a condition imposed by the Incorporated Society, who made a grant of £225 towards the building. The organ seen here was installed in 1889.

James Hodkinson, who, as a young man in 1853, assisted the first clerk of Bitterne Parish church, a Mr Liney. He was present at the ceremonies of laying the foundation stone and at the consecration of the church; he was the first lad to be confirmed there. He succeeded Mr Liney as clerk in 1863 and held the post for sixty-four years. His brother, Edward, was his assistant for thirty-six years. When he retired in 1927, he was succeeded by his grandson, A.T.J. Hodkinson (Tom), who still held the position at the church's centenary in 1953. The current clerk is Paul Hodkinson, Tom's son. Thus the story of the first Bitterne Parish clerks is virtually that of one family, with a wonderful record of over 140 years faithful service.

'Bossy' the donkey, seen here in Bitterne churchyard, c. 1975. He was the pet of the Revd Michael Perry and his family and made guest appearances in some church services, particularly at Christmas and Palm Sunday. The Revd Perry came to Bitterne as curate in 1968 and was made vicar in 1972. He was a talented musician and, whilst at Bitterne, composed many hymns and choruses, of which the most popular was the *Calypso Carol*. He left Bitterne for the smaller parish of Eversley so that he could concentrate on his writing. Sadly, he died of cancer in 1997.

Bitterne 2850 Company Church Lads Brigade annual camp on the Sussex coast, *c.* 1910. From left to right, standing: Eric Haynes, Dick Collins, Jeff Jeffries, Fred Brewer, Stan Hammerton. Kneeling: Albert Burgess. Sitting: Bill Moody, Bert Cowley, Charlie Shepherd. The Church Lads Brigade met at the Mission Hall under the leadership of Captain Brewer.

The first anniversary of the Young Wives on the vicarage lawn in 1947. It is still a popular venue for summer fêtes. The Victorian vicarage was demolished in 1969, when part of the grounds were sold to the Methodists for their new church, providing funds for a modern house.

Bitterne Covenanters 1969/70. Part of a national Anglican youth movement for boys aged thirteen to sixteen, they met on Sunday mornings in the Church Hall under the leadership of Alan Oakley-John. The Girl Covenanters met under the leadership of his wife, Gene, at their home, no. 2 Chessel Avenue. When Alan Oakley-John retired as a GP, he and his wife became missionaries in Juba (Southern Sudan), ministering both medically and pastorally to people devastated by famine and civil war. They returned to live in Bitterne in 1982 and Oakley-John Walk is named after 'Doc John'.

The Church Institute, c. 1938. It was completed in the autumn of 1932, on the site of the present church hall. In 1941, after it had been taken over for Civil Defence purposes, it was burnt out by an incendiary bomb. Fortunately, the crockery had been stored in the vicarage and was in regular use for many decades afterwards.

The corner of Marne Road and Commercial Street, with the Mission Hall on the left, c. 1900. It was built as Bitterne's first infants' school in 1857, paid for by the Revd Henry Usborne and his sister. It was sold in 1897, when the Queen Victoria School opened, and became a Gospel Hall. It was rebuilt in the 1960s.

A group outside the Mission Hall, including: Bert James, Mrs Elsie Brown, J. James, Mrs Rita Gardiner, Mr James Snr and Mrs R. James.

The funeral hearse of Sarah Adcock at Hedge End, 24 October 1912. The costs were £3 12s 6d for the funeral and 7/- for the grave. Pictured here on the hearse are: Mr R. Payne (both Senior and Junior), Mr Fancy, Mr Martin, Mr Fisher and Mr King.

The funeral procession, on 12 May 1927, of 'Honest John' Brown of no. 29 Dean Road, seen from Boyes Bakery and showing the Drill Hall and the Red Lion. He was much respected as the chairman of the Parish council, Councillor for Bitterne and Sholing Ward and a trustee of the Bitterne Wesleyan Methodist church. He worked in a local brick works until 1890, when he became a wharfinger in Southampton Docks, rising to the position of quayside foreman. The total cost of the funeral, including horse and carriage, flowers and six bearers for the coffin, was £14 3s 0d.

Six
Entertainment
and Sport

In the days before radio, the cinema, television and the Internet, entertainment was very much a DIY affair. A piano was an essential part of the home furniture and members of the family often played various other instruments or sang unaccompanied. Fêtes and carnivals were also a regular feature of Bitterne Village life, participated in with great enthusiasm. Outside entertainments, such as the circus or other travelling amusements, were avidly patronised, and all sporting activities, of which there were many, received very strong support.

A portion of land in Bitterne Road, near the corner of Commercial Street, called 'The Hampshire', was a favourite stopping place for travelling fairs, and this itinerant 'Freak and Novelty Show' was a great attraction for the locals. The lady seated in front of her substantial motor caravan is Miss Rose Foster. Born at Southampton in around 1888, she was only twenty-six inches tall, being born without arms or legs. She could nevertheless write, knit and dress herself. To make an independent living, she was obliged to exhibit herself, extravagantly advertising as 'Nature's strangest mistake' and 'The eighth wonder of the world'. She travelled widely with Barnum & Bailey and Ringling Brothers shows and 'on four occasions appeared before the Crowned Heads of Europe'. After that, Bitterne must have seemed rather a let-down for her....

Bitterne Cricket Club, at the Veracity Ground, c.1875. The Bitterne team struggled to make an impression at this time, being eclipsed by local rivals West End, who got the better of them. The scorer on the left, with the bowler hat and beard, is the great-great grandfather of Mr R.C. Payne, Bitterne's well-known undertaker. Also included in the picture are Messrs Candy, Batt, W. Cross and Albert Whitlock.

Bitterne Cricketers, in the grounds of Harefield House, c. 1920. Included in the picture are Messrs Ball, Macham, Sly, Small, Gould, Fry, Miller, Bailey, Freemantle, Fisher, Wiltshire, A. Whitlock, F. Whitlock, P. Batt, A.Gadd, J. Gadd and E. Gadd. Cricket in Bitterne can be traced back to the mid-1800s, with a number of teams taking the Bitterne name. Matches played in the last century often attracted large crowds, who enhanced their enjoyment of the game by holding parties and generally consuming alcohol.

A 100-yard ladies' race, held at the Bitterne Conservative and Unionist Association sports fête at Brownlow Park, the home of Mr and Mrs Jack Bucknill, 11 August 1913. Bitterne Local History Society has a number of postcards of this event in its collection, including 'The Crowd' and 'The Greasy Pole Competition'.

The 100-yards skipping race, at the same event. Pictured are: John Shapland (extreme right), Bert Tomes (at the rear, marked with a cross) and John Russell (centre, in a straw hat).

No. 5 Brook Road, decorated for the Bitterne Carnival, early 1900s. The house won first prize, which was richly deserved for the amount of effort that had been put into it. The expense of these elaborate decorations, relative to the (very probable) low income of the household, demonstrates the great enthusiasm for the carnival by residents at this period.

Bitterne Carnivals were well attended: this group, at the top of Dean Road, has attracted a good crowd of children, *c.* 1910. Before the First World War, the Bitterne Carnival was an eagerly awaited diversion. The colourful procession would wend its way around the village, headed by local bandsmen, reaching a triumphant climax when it came to the Brownlow grounds, where Bartlett's roundabouts and swings, coconut shies and hoopla would be waiting. A 'battle of confetti' often took place and there was dancing until midnight.

An ingenious carnival entry, *c.* 1910. The 'youngest lady aviator in the world' was marked up to 'descend 7.15 tonight at Brownlow'. The area played a major part in the early development of aviation, under the patronage of enthusiasts such as Lord Swaythling and Hubert Scott-Paine. One wonders if the young lady got to fly.

The National Deposit Friendly Society (West End district) carnival float at Bitterne Sports Ground, Wynter Road. This society was established in 1868, the West End branch opening in around 1932. It had branches throughout the Southampton area, including Bitterne, Woolston, Itchen and Sholing.

Public houses always had a good supply of regulars who were prepared to organise group activities. This crowd outside the John Barleycorn in Commercial Street are clearly having an enjoyable party. It is highly improbable that the police sergeant is genuine!

Corks was a popular inter-public house game, played by placing five specially shaped corks on a table, the smallest in the centre. Three corks, called 'bungs', were used (from about nine feet away) to knock down as many corks as possible with three throws. This team won the 1912 Bitterne and West End league. Included amongst the group pictured outside the Percy Arms are: Bill Boncey, Bill Young, Harry Smith, Walt Bailey, Fred Grant, Gus Dunsby, Alec Cardy, Harry Dunsby, Edgar and Fred Cardy.

Mrs Ventham's concert party, *c.* 1923. Amongst those in attendance are: Norman Shapland, Len Steer, Mrs Ventham, Margaret Grundy, Hector Steer, Alec Shapland, Veronica Dowty, Margaret Griffin, Winnie Haskell, Marjorie Ventham, Olive Mist, Harold Watson, Mary Dowty, Arthur Ventham, Jane Ventham and Hector Prickett and sisters. They rehearsed in the drill hall and performed, amongst other places, at Netley Hospital, for soldiers wounded in the First World War.

Between the wars, Mr Malizia, an Italian organ grinder, used to walk from Southampton and Woolston to play in Bitterne. The family were also well known for their ice-cream, which they sold from gaily decorated barrows. He is seen here in the High Street, with the Congregational church on the right, in around 1930.

A Southampton Corporation horse dressed for May Day at Oak Lodge, Freemantle Common Road. This building was at one time the Southampton Corporation depot, with stabling for the Corporation horses. It is currently used by Social Services.

Tryermayne circulating library, Bitterne Road, c. 1933. The gentleman standing outside is Mr Thomas J. Trethewy. The shop took its name from the adjoining premises, formerly the home of Admiral Thomas Martin. This imposing house, which is still standing, had a large picture window on the west side that gave an uninterrupted panoramic view across Lances Hill to Southampton and beyond.

Bitterne Bowling Club has been playing on the green adjacent to the parish church since 1933. It has always been renowned for its friendly atmosphere and fine sandwiches! The club has achieved much success and still flourishes today. The original Hampshire County Police station is in the background, on the right, and 'Southern Haye' – once Bitterne's vicarage – is on the left.

Bitterne Road Cycling Club, *c.* 1936. They were noted for their friendly and jovial atmosphere, as well as having a record of intense competition. Bert Gatehouse was an influential member who helped develop the local cycle polo league, which played at Bitterne Sports Ground in Wynter Road. The club also embarked on several long distance journeys, covering hundreds of miles. Some members even cycled to Blackpool just to hear Reginald Dixon play the organ!

The Bitterne Nomads, founded in 1939, had a ground in Cutbush Lane and became a prominent local football club. Don Roper played for them as a sixteen-year old, before going on to play for Southampton and Arsenal, where he gained two Championship medals. The Nomads played regularly in the Hampshire League and their biggest achievement was to win the Southampton Senior Cup. Their name is perpetuated in 'Nomad Close', a road on the West End Park estate, which was built over their ground.

Thornycroft (Woolston) Football Club at their home ground, the Veracity Ground, 1922/23 season. The Veracity Ground is now a public open space, with no indication that it had a large grandstand and was once a venue for football matches that attracted crowds of several thousand. A successful FA Cup run saw Thornycroft drawn to play Burnley in 1920, but Burnley protested that the Veracity Ground was unsuitable, so the match took place at Fratton Park, Portsmouth.

A 1953 Coronation party in Commercial Street, photographed by H.J. Morgan of no. 99 Bursledon Road. Note the Mew Langton board outside the Commercial Inn and Lanes Bakery premises opposite. Included in the picture are Mrs Moon and Miss Knight.

The Ritz cinema, Bitterne Road, opened on 28 October 1936. Seating 800, it was a good, family-type cinema, showing films that had a wide appeal. It closed on 1 July 1961, to be demolished and replaced by the present bowling alley. The last Saturday morning show was attended by 600 children. The last film shown was a Republic Picture Corporation production, *The Last Command* – a western starring Ernest Borgnine.

Alan Hopkins on his specially adapted bicycle in the Peartree and Woolston Carnival of 1951. He was advertising the well-known bicycle shop 'Sports', run by Mr A.R. Davies, on the corner of Bitterne Road and West End Road.

Note the poster showing Diana Dors on this 1960 carnival float of Broomfield and Gatehouse, Bitterne moped and motorcycle dealers.

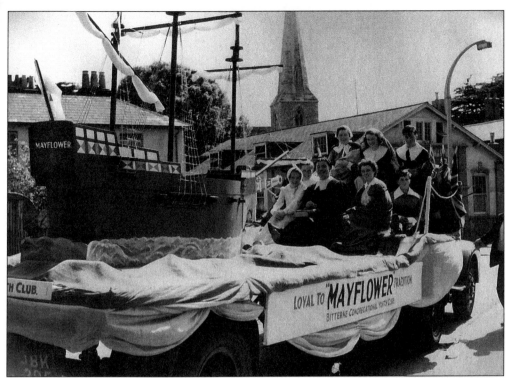

Congregational Church Youth Club entry for the Southampton Carnival, *c.* 1953. The float was built by Bob Payne and Capt. Tom McAllen rigged the ship 'ready for sailing'. On the float are: Margaret Hare, Paddy Wilton, Tony Snow, Roy Haynes and Patsy Ramshaw.

The Bitterne Scout group has always been active within the community. In the 1970s, the Cub Scout section entered elaborate and complex floats in the Southampton Carnival. This one displayed a lunar landscape, with the Cubs dressed as tics and bugs – the mock-up of Dr Who's Tardis disguised a portable toilet (carnival days are long for eight-year olds). The leaders here are Jennie Upton (on left) and Marianne Jupe, who both relinquished their roles in 1995 – Jennie after more than thirty years' outstanding service to the Scout movement.

Bitterne Carnival was revived in 1988, after a lapse of many years. Because of the complication of busy roads, subways and a precinct, it was a 'walking' carnival, following the same pattern as those held in the early part of the century. Note the new shop units to let, under the United Reformed church, and Bitterne Parade (boarded up on the right).

Bitterne Carnival in June 1989 raised £800 for local charities. This Bitterne Local History Society entry on the theme of 'Summertime Fun' won first prize in its class; the banner was made by members June and Keith Ellwood.

Seven

Wartime

Patriotism has always been a strong feature of English village life. Losses in action frequently appeared massive in proportion to the size of the community. In the First World War, fifty-two men from Bitterne gave their lives (out of a total population of about 3,000). Their names, along with those of the forty-three who died in the Second World War, are displayed in the parish church. The Armed Forces have invariably been well supported by volunteers from Bitterne, with the local drill hall providing useful training facilities. The First World War saw the local gentry frequently throwing open their homes and/or grounds to entertain servicemen returning from the Front. It also saw many thousands of troops spending the night in Bitterne before their cross-channel journey to France: they slept in schools, churches and in private houses. The Second World War brought conflict actually into Bitterne, which suffered as a result of its proximity to the Spitfire factory and the port area of Southampton, both being prime targets for aerial attacks. Those not in the Forces also played their part in local defence and the auxiliary services, displaying great heroism.

Taken from a painting of the Red Lion Cut presented to Winifred Hammett at Bitterne School as first prize in a race, this picture shows the original wooden drill hall, used for military training for many years. It dated from about 1880.

Staff and patients at Sydney House Hospital *c.* 1915. The hospital stood at the junction of Peartree Avenue and Freemantle Common Road and, for many years, was owned and occupied by the Ede family. Following subsequent demolition of the house, the grounds were used for some fifty years by Southampton Corporation to accommodate their Parks Nurseries.

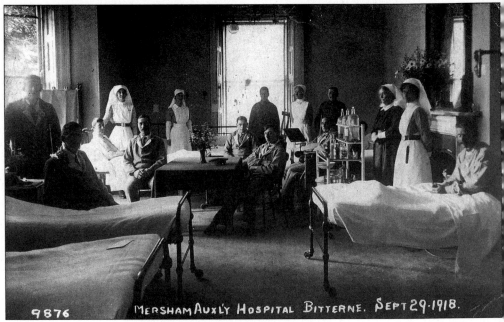

Mersham Auxiliary Hospital, Bitterne, September 1918. Many of the large houses in the area, like Mersham, became temporary hospitals and convalescent homes during the First World War. The site is now occupied by Mersham Gardens.

Women 'did their bit' in the First World War by relieving the country's chronic manpower shortage in many areas. In March 1915, the Government set up a Register of Women for War Service, enabling them to sign on at their local labour exchange. This was warmly welcomed by Emmeline Pankhurst, leader of the women's suffrage movement. The Osman ladies – daughters of Thomas and Elizabeth Osman of no. 44 Brook Road – are here seen dressed for their Land Army duties in around 1916. They are, from left to right: Nancy and Maud (at rear), Victoria and Alexandria.

This group of soldiers, dutifully posing for the camera during the First World War in the grounds of Bitterne Manor House (see page 26), were evidently being entertained to tea there by Miss Lettice MacNaghten. The eldest daughter of Sir Steuart and Lady Amy MacNaghten, she continued living there until 1939.

The Royal Hampshire Regiment, which proudly held many battle honours, played a significant part in the First World War, including heroic action at the bloody battles of Ypres and Gallipoli, where losses were frighteningly high. It was well served with men from the Bitterne area. The gallant troops, seen here in 1917, are, from left to right: Alfred Benjamin Michael Betts (from Deacon Road), Robert Lewis Heath (from Manor Road), and 'Tosher' Lawrence of Spring Road.

Armistice Day 1918, on the vicarage lawn in Bursledon Road. On the platform are, from left to right, Revd Vincett Cook (Congregational), Revd Arthur Crocket and Councillor John Brown.

Peace celebrations on Peartree Green, 1919. The group includes George Cude. The war ended on 11 November 1918, but peace celebrations awaited Germany's acceptance of the Treaty of Versailles on 28 June 1919. Local celebrations went on into July.

Bitterne peace celebrations on the Harefield estate, with Reuben Cleverley and his daughter Rose (Puntis), together with Eva Spencer, Bert Elliot, Bert Cowley, Bill Smith and Dusty Miller. The horse, named 'Kitty', was wounded in France and subsequently bought by Mr Cleverley.

In 1896, Mr Adcock, grocer of Alma (later Almatade) Road, let his shed to the Bitterne Fire Brigade, led by Captain Moody, to store their appliance for £5 a year. The solid hinges of the sturdy gates are still visible today. The Captain and his stalwart crew, including Miller, Brewer, two Whitlocks, Bishop, Payne and Barrett, are pictured there in around 1906. Fire cover in the Bitterne area at this time consisted of a hand cart and nine firemen.

Fire Engine No. 8 at Woolston Fire Station in September 1939. The driver is Bill (Tiny) Vickers, who is next to Leading Fireman Edgar Grigg. Other crew members are: Bill Cole, Len Wicks and Bert Instone. The station was vacated and the crews transferred to Hightown in January 1996. The premises have since been converted into 'The Old Fire Station Surgery' for a group medical practice.

Major Kendall collecting salvage in Thornhill Park Road, c. 1940. This was part of his contribution to the war effort. Materials of all kinds were salvaged at this period, not, as is the case today, for 'green' purposes, but to reduce the need for imports by ships that had to run the gauntlet of German U-boats.

The ARP Wardens of Post 3, Beech Avenue, c. 1940. The full team consisted of: Mr Buxey, Mr Woods, F. Calton Jnr, Miss Cox, K. Poole, Miss Bresher, Jean Brown, Mr Taylor, Mr Cox, Mr Doling, Mr Sainsbury, Mr Yeomans and Mr Calton Snr, with messengers Ken Davis, K. Deane and J. Davis. Jean Brown (without uniform) was later to wear her Girls' Brigade uniform in lieu of the correct ARP one.

On 14 May 1940, the Government asked for volunteers, initially called the Local Defence Volunteers, to oppose possible landings by German parachutists. After the first week of the appeal, 400,000 had volunteered and by the end of the war the total reached 1.8 million! The Bitterne Home Guard, seen here, was formed on 7 April 1941, under the command of Capt. Jack Wheatley (not in the picture). The group includes Norman Brown and Norman and Alf Gardiner. It was part of the Bitley Company, so named after the areas east of the River Itchen, compounded from Bitterne and Botley.

An image showing the suburban impact of German high explosive bombs during the raids of November and December, 1940. No. 251 Bitterne Road, adjacent to the old Lances Hill Toll House (to its right), was badly damaged but repairable.

Railway communications were obvious targets for the Luftwaffe and the lines following the east bank of the River Itchen must have been easy targets to locate. Workmen are seen here repairing bomb-damaged tracks at Bitterne in June 1942.

'Victory in Europe' was a joyous occasion, here being celebrated in Court Close, Milbury Crescent, on 8 May 1945. In the crowd are Frances and Robert Hammon, Paddy Fulford, Alan, Christine, and Marion Dyer, G. Risewood, Thelma Matthews, Derek House, Jean and Peter Watton.

The British Legion Fête Committee, at Bitterne Sports Ground, Wynter Road, August 1949. The pavilion in the background came from the First World War No. 1 British Red Cross Hospital, at Netley. This was a large temporary hospital, composed of many huts, located behind the Royal Victoria Military Hospital alongside Southampton Water.

Bitterne's original wooden drill hall (see page 95) was replaced in around 1910 by this substantial brick building. It served as the base for the Hampshire 1st Volunteer Brigade (No. 6 Company) of the Southern Division, Royal Artillery, until they moved to larger premises in 1939. During the Second World War, it was used as a temporary fire station and subsequently had several uses, mainly light engineering, before being demolished in 1982.

The war destroyed many Southampton homes, some of which the Council replaced with prefabricated concrete and aluminium bungalows and houses, known as 'pre-fabs'. Those shown here are in Barnes Close, looking towards Bitterne Road, with the new Harefield Council estate in the background. Many pre-fab bungalows were replaced with brick housing in the 1960s, but most of the houses still remain, despite being 'temporary' when built.

More pre-fabs, this time in Montgomery Road on the Bitterne Lodge estate, with an Anderson air-raid shelter being used as a garden shed, a very common adaptation after the war. Anderson shelters were originally set deep into the ground with several feet of earth on top to provide protection against anything other than a direct hit. After the war, many residents took the opportunity to purchase their shelter to use as a garden shed.

The Decontamination Unit at the north end of Freemantle Common, for use in the event of a gas attack. It became a day nursery after the war, until eventually being demolished in the 1970s.

Houses that were not completely ruined by bombing were repaired. This semi-detached cottage on the corner of Marne Road and Commercial Street, photographed in June 1994, is a good example – the left-hand side having been completely destroyed. Walter Kingston, of Pound Street, Bitterne, kept a diary of air-raids on Southampton. His entry for 26 September 1940 recalls: 'One wave of bombers accompanied by many fighters suddenly appeared and dived on the Supermarine [Spitfire-producing factory at Woolston] district. The ground and shelters actually swayed from the falling bombs. This had hardly passed when a second attack started. Direct hits on the Supermarine Works and 7 bombs on Whites Yard, Southampton Gasworks hit and along the waterfront. Woolston again badly hit. Bombs in Peartree Avenue. Houses demolished in Marne [including no. 21, the missing half of this originally semi-detached pair] and Balaclava Roads, Bitterne, and in the Convent grounds. Many craters in the river bed at low tide'.

Eight
Transport

The deep valleys of the area, and the eventual progression to mechanised transport, has affected the nature of Bitterne's communications. The horse was, of course, essential in the early nineteenth century, and the lovely carriages of the local gentry became almost an art form. While people walked to work, or to shop, the steep inclines created problems for transporting bulk goods. Extra horses were available at the bottom of Lances Hill in case of difficulty and wedges were kept on the hill to put behind cart wheels to give the horses a rest. The first public transport to and from Bitterne was a horse-drawn coach which, during the 1840s, ran four times a day to its terminus at no. 132 High Street, Southampton. In 1859, Amos Rockett started a mail, omnibus and carrier service to Southampton, which operated twice daily. His family continued the carrier service until well into the 1930s. The advent of the 'horse-less carriage' at the end of the century did not initially overcome the steep gradients. The first Southampton Corporation bus service to these areas (linking with the floating bridge) did not commence until 9 November 1920; on 15 December 1920 the Hants & Dorset Bus Company began a service through Bitterne on its Bishops Waltham route. Electric trams and the railway were also prevented, by the gradients, from running in the immediate vicinity of Bitterne Village.

This carriage belonged to Mr H. Whicher, a 'jobmaster' of Angel Mews, High Street, Bitterne. Lances Hill was much steeper in the days of horse transport than it is now, so horses were grateful for a break and a drink when they reached the top. The trough was erected through local public subscription in 1905 by the Metropolitan Drinking Fountain and Cattle Trough Association. It originally had another trough underneath, for 'hot dogs'! It now stands as a feature at the end of the pedestrian precinct – a reminder of yesteryear.

This lovely carriage, pictured in May 1925, is driven by Albert Henry Adcock, a shopkeeper of No. 15 Alma Road, Bitterne. He was known locally as 'Gentleman Adcock'.

Miss Caroline Maud Coote, (daughter of Admiral Coote and known as Maud) of Shales, West End Road, pictured with her horse, Cormac, c. 1884. The estate had a plentiful supply of carriages in the days before the automobile became popular.

Jasper Thomas Dear, a fishmonger, who was born in Poole in 1885 and lived at no. 52 Chapel Street (Dean Road), with his daughter Winnie. The picture was taken on 15 July 1925, in front of Charlie Mist's bootmakers, No. 50 Chapel Street.

This horse bus is pictured soon after 1898, when Southampton Corporation took over the Southampton Tramways Company. This service continued until August 1902, when it was replaced by the electric trams. 'To and from Bitterne Park Estate' meant terminating at Bitterne Park Triangle, the service running via the 'free' Cobden Bridge to Southampton (opened in 1883).

The electric tram route to Bitterne Park Triangle opened on Saturday 30 August 1902 and was extended down Bullar Road to Bitterne railway station on 26 July 1923. The trams were in use for the next twenty-five years, until the route east of Portswood closed on 15 May 1948. This picture of a 'knife-board' central seating tram was taken as it travelled towards Cobden Bridge.

A Corporation tramcar at the bottom of Bullar Road, the terminus from the town via Portswood and Cobden Bridge. The Northam terminus was at the town side of Northam Bridge, as it could not be crossed by tram. Trams were withdrawn from the Bullar Road route on 16 May 1948 and replaced by Corporation buses.

This is thought to be the first omnibus serving Bitterne and Woolston, c. 1923. The first Southampton Corporation bus service to these areas (serving the floating bridge) commenced on 9 November 1920. It was suspended on 15 January 1921, because of the poor condition of the road surfaces, but re-opened on 7 September 1922. The service was extended to Sholing on 3 June 1926.

The Chessel bus, pictured here on 26 January 1954, travelled from central Southampton to Woolston via Chessel Avenue and was the only route that served Peartree Avenue. Negotiating the hills to Bitterne when snow is about is never easy! A single-deck bus had to be used to pass under the railway bridge in Bridge Road, Woolston.

Bill Shepherd of Dean Road, with 'his' Southampton Corporation steamroller. He had the contract for surfacing the road from Northam Bridge through Bitterne to Botley. BLHS member Mildred Russell vividly recalls him driving the steamroller along Dean Road, because he was allowed to bring it home and park it outside his house at night. When he retired, in around 1950, the Corporation offered him the steamroller for nothing, but his wife refused to have it in the garden!

A converted 'Pagefield' lorry, made in Wigan and owned by Bitterne Motor Works, outside their garage (which later became Guster's shop). The coachwork was by Bitterne craftsmen and the upholstery by staff of Edwin Jones' department store. The shop premises of Miss Heath's confectioners can be seen in the background.

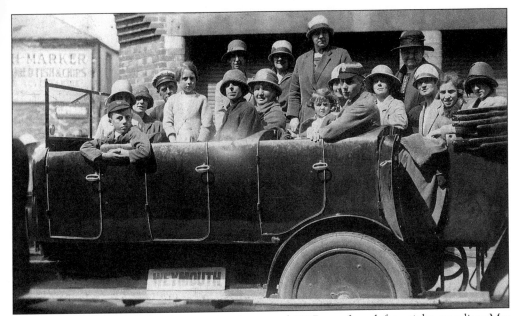

Enjoying a Whites Road charabanc outing, in around 1927, are, from left to right, standing: Mrs Symes, Mrs Payne, Mrs T. Macham, Mrs Brett (the little girl is Vera Harris). Sitting: ? Dumper (the boy), -?-, Hilda Harris, -?- (driver), Mrs Harris, Mrs Butt, ? Dumper (small child), Mrs Dumper, M. Macham (wearing the old style Taunton School cap), Mrs C. Macham, Mrs Parker, Kath Butt and Mrs Dunsby.

A 'Queen' charabanc, *c.* 1921. It is outside the Red Lion Hotel, whose landlord at that time was F.W. Trownson. A common destination for outings was the Chedder Caves and westerly journeys involved a refreshment stop at Salisbury. The vehicle was a solid tyre 'Dennis' charabanc, which was limited to 12 mph. Photographs of charabancs in the BLHS collection invariably show them with an open top – as though the weather was consistently good!

Another of the (very popular) charabanc outings, probably from the Angel Inn, *c.* 1923. Amongst the passengers are: Len Martin, Mr Vare, Mr Rogers and girls, Cliff Godwin, G.H. Gould (standing), Mrs Vare (with baby), Mr and Mrs Rockett, Mrs Austin, Mrs Gould, Grannie Godwin, Mr and Mrs A. Whitlock.

An outing from the Commercial Inn, *c.* 1932. This was arranged by the Hampshire Friendly Society. The group includes: Mr and Mrs Wells; Mrs Nimmins and son; Mrs Miller and Freda; Mrs Boulton and Chris; Mrs Berry and Jack, Ivy, Vera and Gwen; Mrs Palmer, Russell and Kathleen; Mrs Shepherd and Alf, Betty and Gwen; Mrs Reeves, Leslie and John.

Opened as Bitterne Road Station in March 1866, its name was changed to Bitterne Station in 1896. The Southampton to Netley railway was originally a single track with a passing loop here at Bitterne. Seen here, on the left, is the 'up' platform (towards Southampton). As the railway company did not deliver to Bitterne, a contract was awarded to an agent, Mr Rockett of Pound Street. The goods yard closed in July 1959.

The train now standing at Bitterne Station is a British Rail standard class 4 4-6-0. Electric lighting had replaced the gas lamps that were in use at the station until 1968. The signal box closed on 10 October 1966 and was demolished in 1969. The station is at the bottom of Lances Hill, a mile from Bitterne Village.

Steam engines were technically innovatory and a complete contrast to the traction engine design. Garrett's produced the first rigid six-wheel undertypes in 1926 and these had a 12-15 ton capacity. This Garrett steam wagon was owned by Fairway Garage, at the junction of Bullar Road and Bitterne Road. At one time it was a petrol filling station, also selling spare parts and carrying out repairs, but it became difficult to negotiate the complex roads system that developed around the area and the garage closed.

The Revd A. Crockett, c. 1919. He was vicar of Bitterne from 1908 until 1920. Although he is wearing the mortarboard in fun as part of the 1919 peace celebrations, he was entitled to it as a Master of Arts. He was reputed to be a vigorous preacher, whose clear and forceful voice kept his parishioners alert throughout his rather lengthy sermons.

A Triumph Dolomite car, owned by Gordon Stan Emmence – 'mine host' at the Red Lion from around 1939 until 1957 – seen outside his premises. Gordon was also a greyhound trainer, with quarters at Steventon Manor near Basingstoke.

Bitterne Cab Company was started with three taxis (later increased to five) by Tom Misselbrook on 9 May 1945, on the site of the present Roman Catholic church. It was originally called Bitterne Hire Service. Shortly afterwards, Mr Cartwright, who ran a taxi from his home in Mousehole Lane, registered the same name for himself, so Tom immediately changed his to Bitterne Road Hire. In 1953, Tom concentrated on his car sales business, which he had started in 1938, and sold the taxis to his drivers. The firm continues to this day, as the Bitterne Cab Company, at no. 10 Deacon Road.

Mr H.C. White with his New Imperial. He ran the boot and shoe warehouse in Lion Place from 1925 until 1957. It was started in 1887 by his uncle, Mr T. J. Stokes, and was in the same family for seventy years, in the days when the owner worked in his shop and service was more personal than in today's multiple stores. Mr White built up a reputation for good quality boots and shoes and for satisfaction in the repair side of the business.

Promoting Dunlop National Tyre Week, 1960. Bert Gatehouse worked for Sports cycle shop at the top of Lances Hill for several years before joining forces with Ted Broomfield in this shop at the corner of Almatade Road and Commercial Street.

Nine

The Main Road

Bitterne's first known main road was a Roman one, Route 421, leading from Clausentum (Bitterne Manor) to Chichester. Its existence was confirmed during excavations on Freemantle Common in July 1968 and is marked by a plaque. At the end of the eighteenth century, Bitterne was sparsely populated, with a few scattered estates and otherwise barren common land. The scene changed significantly following the construction, in 1799, of a bridge between Northam and Bitterne Manor, with a new road leading to Botley. This placed Bitterne on a main road, relieving its comparative isolation and stimulating the growth of a village at the top of the hill. Another road was constructed in 1801, leading to a new bridge over the River Hamble at Bursledon. It joined the Botley road at Bitterne, forming the now famous 'Bitterne Fork'. These roads, connecting the towns of Southampton and Portsmouth, created a commercial route as well as opening up the Bitterne area. The main road (High Street) through Bitterne became the hub of the community that evolved. However, these routes were privately owned, with toll gates, making the village still somewhat isolated – much of the cross-country traffic used the Swaythling-Botley Road and thus avoided Bitterne entirely. The situation changed significantly when the area became part of Southampton in 1920, followed in 1929 by the ending of road tolls.

The Bitterne Fork, c. 1895. Albert Terrace in Bursledon Road is on the right and High Street, with Lankester and Crook in the background, on the left. Mr J. Eden, landlord of the Red Lion, is in his garden and everybody in view appears to be posing for the photographer.

High Street, looking west towards Southampton from the junction with Commercial Street, *c.* 1890. Lion Place is on the left and the shops of J.A. Russell (furniture), 'Spitty' Smith (hairdresser) and J. Levy (fishmonger) can be seen. The lion can just be seen on the roof.

High Street, looking east towards Thornhill from the junction with Maytree Road, *c.* 1890. Pound Street is on the left. Mr G. Gould Snr, one of the local undertakers, stands at the left-hand side of the picture. The Red Lion is in the distance. Bitterne House (later called 'The Old House'), 'Maytree' and 'Monte Repos' can be seen on the right.

Lances Hill, named after David Lance, the original owner of Chessel House (see page 28), looking west towards Southampton, c. 1905. Alf Rockett, the agent for the LSWR, is in his cart on a journey from the village to the station. On the right-hand side of the road you can see the logs that were put behind the cart wheels to give horses a rest on the steep climb.

Lances Hill, c. 1905. The stile led up to Monks' Path, leading to Bitterne Grove, and is now the entrance to Glenfield Avenue. Little Lances Hill is on the right. At this period, Lances Hill was much shorter and steeper than it is today. Its gradient has been twice modified, first in the 1920s and again in the 1950s. Near the summit, the houses are today perched on a high bank, whilst around the base of the hill the gardens are well below road level.

Guy's Cottage, on the extreme left, looking east along Bitterne Road, *c.* 1905. The nearby gable-ended building served as a Brethren meeting place, in which the Boyes family, from the adjoining bakery, were very active. Note, on the right, the distinctive 'stink-pipe' for ventilating the sewer system. The sender of this postcard asked the recipient if he already possessed 'this beautiful view'.

The first Lances Hill Toll Gate in its original position, *c.* 1905. The thatched cottage was an entrance lodge to the Chessel Estate, at this period owned by William Henry Richardson, who was well known for his generosity to local people in need. After his death, in 1906, the house stood empty until 1910, when the estate was sold for housing development.

The Lances Hill Toll Gate, seen across the road in the background of this photograph from around 1910, has now been moved up the hill, past the junction with Midanbury Lane on the left. Development of the land immediately north of the road meant that the toll-gate could be avoided. Consequently, it was moved twice, each time westwards up Lances Hill.

The final position of the Lances Hill Toll Gate, c. 1925. The toll keeper's house is on the left. This still stands today, albeit with a much shortened porch, near the corner of Glenfield Avenue.

The Thornycroft six-wheel Southampton Corporation bus, in its navy blue and cream livery, carries local dignitaries in 1929, when the Lances Hill toll gate was removed. The vacant plots on the right were developed over the ensuing decade into the present Glenfield Avenue and Crescent.

Celebrating the freeing of the Lances Hill toll, outside the Red Lion Hotel on 16 May 1929. Present are Aldmermen Blakeway, Sidney Kimber (later Sir), Dunsford, Brown and Bagshaw; Councillors Dixey, Sanders, Young; Mrs M. Godwin, Mr Southwell, Revd Basil S. Aldwell, Mr Pugh (the mayor), R. Meggeson (the town clerk) and Mrs Bucknell.

Many Bitterne road names were changed in 1924, following the incorporation into Southampton County Borough in 1920, to end duplication with other roads in the borough. The new name originally proposed for High Street, Bitterne, was Arcadian Road but there were strong objections and the new sign was mysteriously 'tarred and feathered' several times before the Corporation agreed to adopt the name 'Bitterne Road'. The culprits were never caught!

Bitterne Road, looking west towards Southampton, c. 1954. Hornby's dairy on the right has changed to Haytons and Bitterne Parade, which contains Dewhurst's butchers, Glanvilles, Flux, White, Hayton, Lee Garrett and Bollom cleaners. The trees beyond the Methodist church were soon replaced by F.W. Woolworth's and Bitterne's first supermarket, Fine Fare (both now gone), together with some smaller shops.

Bitterne Road on 25 July 1982. The empty shops on the left originally consisted of four cottages, known as 'Albert Place'. The Bitterne Lion is just visible on his lofty perch on top of 'Lion Place' (see page 52).

The Bitterne bypass, looking west from the roof of the new Bitterne police station. Tom Misselbrook's car sales are on the left, but the roads are surprisingly devoid of traffic. The white house on the right still stands (no. 11 Dean Road), a testimony to Mr Diaper (the owner) who argued that its demolition was unnecessary. Originally, it was in the middle of a row of twelve, the other being knocked down to make way for the bypass and leisure centre.

The plinth unveiled by Councillor Ivy White on 23 June 1987, creating a new and distinctive landmark at the site of the former notorious forked junction. The lion originally topped the frontage of a terrace of cottages, built in 1844 in the High Street. *The Hampshire Independent* carried the following advertisement on 7 August 1844: 'To Grocers, Drapers, Tailors, Boot and Shoe Makers, Cabinet-makers, and others. To be let with immediate possession, at low rents, Four newly-erected DWELLING HOUSES, with lofty Modern Shops, fitted with mahogany sashes and occupying frontages of 15 and 18 feet each, facing the Botley Road, in the preferable part of Bittern [sic] and forming the whole of Lion Terrace. The above offer an excellent opportunity to any person wishing to embark in business, and from the great increase of houses and population in this neighbourhood, there is every prospect of success. For a view and terms apply to Mr GURMAN, builder, Bittern [sic], or to Messrs. WITHERS and ROBERTS, Auctioneers, 10 Above Bar, Southampton'.

The Bitterne Lion, in all his new found glory. He was said to get down at night and prowl the village to protect the inhabitants from danger.

Acknowledgements

The illustrations in this book come from the Bitterne Local History Society collection, made available by kind friends and organisations. They are too numerous to mention, but our grateful thanks are extended to them all. We would, however, especially like to thank Southern Newspapers, for permission to use pictures from their archive. The map (on page 2) is reproduced from the 1910 Ordnance Survey map, licence number MC 87935M. The compilation team of Ian Abrahams, Jim Brown, Eddie Croxson, Keith Marsh and Richard Sheaf are also indebted for the invaluable contributions of Jack Hasler, Joan Holt, Aubrey Robertson, Mildred Russell and, most especially, Alan G.K. Leonard. If we have inadvertently infringed anybody's rights in respect of photographic reproduction in theses pages, the compilers and publisher hope they will be excused. Other Bitterne Local History Society Publications include:

Bitterne Before the By-pass	BLHS	£5.95
Memories of Merry Oak	Reg Ward	£4.95

These titles, along with further details and a range of more than twenty-five local papers (priced from 70p to £4.00), can be obtained by contacting the society. The address is: 37 Brook Road, Bitterne Village, Southampton, Hampshire SO18 6AZ. Alternatively, you can look at the website at: www.bitterne2.freeserve.co.uk.